"Kenneth Steven is a bard in the richest and fullest sense of the word. His poems are incantations, invocations of the Divine Presence in the wild places of the Highlands and in our hearts and souls. We do not read his words so much as find ourselves invited to inhabit them."
—Carl McColman, author of *Eternal Heart*

"A pulse of something rare, quiet, and holy beats in the heart of these poems—call it the seasons turning in his beloved Scotland, call it a lyrical voice addressing and blessing this poet's beloved recognition of the gifts of this earth, which he gives back so generously to us. In 'Stopping To See' he tells us 'You are blown out, / have gone beyond all clocks and watches / ink a place where only being matters.' And, indeed, these poems touch and dwell in the sacredness of pure presence, which is a miraculous and even deeper gift that puts us in touch with eternity. Only by books like this is our humanity fully revealed and redeemed."
—Robert D. Vivian, author of *Cold Snap As Yearning* and *The Least Cricket Of Evening* and Professor of English, Alma College

IONA

New and Selected Poems

KENNETH STEVEN

PARACLETE PRESS
BREWSTER, MASSACHUSETTS

2021 First Printing

Iona: New and Selected Poems
Copyright © 2021 by Kenneth Steven
ISBN 978-1-64060-630-2

The Paraclete Press name and logo (dove on cross) are trademarks of Paraclete Press.

Library of Congress Cataloging-in-Publication Data
Names: Steven, Kenneth C., 1968- author.
Title: Iona : new and selected poems / Kenneth Steven.
Description: Brewster, Massachusetts : Paraclete Press, [2021] | Summary:
"These poems are essentially a love song to a precious and extraordinary place, the island of
Iona"-- Provided by publisher.
Identifiers: LCCN 2020049832 (print) | LCCN 2020049833 (ebook) | ISBN
9781640606302 (trade paperback) | ISBN 9781640606319 (epub) | ISBN
9781640606326 (pdf)
Subjects: LCGFT: Poetry.
Classification: LCC PR6069.T444 I58 2021 (print) | LCC PR6069.T444
(ebook) | DDC 821/.914--dc23
LC record available at https://lccn.loc.gov/2020049832
LC ebook record available at https://lccn.loc.gov/2020049833

10 9 8 7 6 5 4 3 2 1

Published by Paraclete Press
Brewster, Massachusetts
www.paracletepress.com

Digitally printed

For Linnie and Rich, with love

Contents

II

III

INTRODUCTION

I grew up in Highland Perthshire, the only truly land-locked part of Scotland—a kind of heartland. There was nature in abundance: rivers, lochs, forests and hills—but no sea. I remember yearning for the sheer sound of the sea again and again in the communities where we lived, but the sea was for summer.

I had a father who was a true outdoorsman, and from earliest days my childhood was composed of exploring woods and climbing hills and visiting high lochs. Saturdays were for the outdoors; Sundays were for church and home. My mother, a Highlander, had grown up in the Free Church, a denomination particularly strict when it came to Sunday observance. For her there could be no "outdooring" then: often as a family we attended two services, on occasion even three.

I counted the days to the summer when I would have the sea once more—and the sea meant always the Atlantic coast. Then we would visit one or other of the Hebridean islands, or perhaps a special corner of the west coast. The jewel in the crown of those west coast islands was Iona. My mother had been taken there on holiday by friends at the time when she was finding faith: the island's beauty and its deep spiritual resonance had a profound impact on her. I suppose we were on Iona every second or third summer: rarely did we stay at the same holiday cottage twice.

What was true of all these Hebridean landfalls was that they were utterly safe havens for children. Often, I would be up and out at five in the morning: running to beaches and searching for treasure. My parents worried about nothing more than barbed wire fences and dangerous tides. These were traditional island worlds, where in my childhood Gaelic was still the language of many homes, and of the church.

Iona was the island to which Columba had come with the Christian faith from Ireland, when the Irish were colonizing that part of the west coast of Scotland and the sea roads were busy with Celtic Christian pilgrims. Iona became a heart-stone in that Celtic Christian story: loud with excited talk and argument, a place where books were copied and ideas hammered out—indeed an island so loud with excited talk and argument that many hermit monks fled to find smaller islands and the loneliness of the desert sea so they might better hear the voice of God. Iona became busier still as Columba's fame grew: in time it would be the island where the Book of Kells was created, the greatest of all the treasures of the Celts.

That is what Iona was, but why should it remain such a cherished destination for thousands of people every day through the summer months? Most are here for a few hours, to see the Abbey, re-built last century by the extraordinary radical theologian George Macleod, who formed the Iona Community. The Abbey is special, beautiful even, but there was something else that entranced me about Iona from earliest days.

It lies in me so deeply I don't precisely know what it is; I just recognize its presence, every bit as much as when I experienced it at four or five years old. Iona is not dissimilar to many another Hebridean landfalls with its gnarled red-grey granite hills, its pure white sands, its little glens of orchids in summer. I have struggled for countless years to work out what that difference is, and still I don't truly know or understand.

All I can say is that whenever I head against the wind to go down to the island's south end, Columba's Bay, where the saint first landed, everything else is blown out of me—where I have been in the last year, what I have written, the talks I have given. And new words come: often I go to Iona feeling that the well of words within me has run dry, and suddenly new things are given to me. Because they feel like gifts: almost invariably a fresh poem will appear scribbled on the page in a few minutes, just as though it has been dictated. And in a way I'm glad I don't know what that endlessly alluring power of Iona is composed of, for it means I keep returning and returning, thirsty to find it again and to know it more fully yet.

Within these pages, I've deliberately put Iona poems at the heart. In a way, the collection represents a single year: the looking forward, the being there, and the looking back. There are a few words concerning places and words in Scots / Gaelic that may need clarification: a short glossary is offered at the close of the third section of poems.

I

FINDING

It is not about going on a particular night in the knowledge of
    finding a foal;
it is the chance of it, the perhaps – the making of time to try.
The struggling up at three in the morning in the strangeness
    of the dark
to get ready in soft voices; the going out into the fields on
    padded feet,
no longer worrying about what tasks have been completed,
    which left undone.
It is about walking together leaving silvery trails, uneven, through
    long lush grass;
about coming at last to the place where you hoped it
    might happen,
for some things are not certain – in this world where almost
    everything
is written down and long decided – and always it has
    been that way.
This water meadow where there is always scent of something
    not quite known;
a bowl made of low hills and round it the ancient trees
    held in the still dark.
However many yards away the foal already trying to hobble
    onto legs ridiculously big,
and she pouring into him all the love that she possesses.
Unselfconsciously and with reverence
it is about kneeling in the long wet grass to watch, to wonder.

STRANGE

It was the matter of a donkey and a journey;
the homelessness of a town loud with strangers,
and the corner of some outhouse by the way
where a mother birthed her child in straw at last.

It was a matter of a star that led
strangers to the strangeness of that place;
and the gifts they brought to leave beside the child
who'd become one day the strangest and most unexpected king.

LISTEN

Silence still lives in the spaces they have not paved;
out of reach of the traffic of an age
that does not sleep, that has forgotten God.
It is somewhere down back roads
where swallows ripple-curve the held air
among blossomings of trees,
where the wind does not need to be.
These are the places to which
one puts one's ear like a child,
for listening is to be a child again –
small enough to understand
what silence means.

THE HARP

Under the burning crumble of the peat
last spring, they found the harp.
A thousand years and more it lay
unsung, the chords taut in buried hands
of Celtic bards. The music curled asleep,
its strings still resin, left full of woods
and sea and birds, like paintings in the earth
and only curlews mourning in a bleary sky above.
They lifted out the harp, a dozen heads
all bent and captured, listening for the sounds
that might lie mute inside – the bones of hands
that once had curled for kings. But all around
were broken promises, the wreckage of the Viking lash
across their history's face. The harp still played –
remembered how to weep.

THE SOMEWHERE ROAD

The car hummed out the dirt track west
and the sun was low, a ball of orange-pink
flickering the trees and fields,
peaching soft the level land,
painting the sudden somewhere of a house,
stranded in a field, deep in a sea of grass.

And every house was still a story, and in the undug fields
were books, whole tomes, untouched, unwritten –
yet I could see their edges, in stray geese and bob-tailed deer,
and in the eyes of those who stopped beside the road
to smile, their faces made of light.

LUSKENTYRE

I thought of the word *Luskentyre* –
how it was made of salt and water:
this place of beaches in great white miles,
where light comes chasing like a child,
where sea is neither blue nor green,
but something somewhere in between.
Where summer comes alive at last,
in orchids opening to blow once more
and a whole sky sings with larks.

PAINTING

They went down to the edge of the shore together,
the man and the boy –
the grandfather and the ten-year-old,
the farmer and the child
with hair the colour of ripe horse chestnuts.
They went with the beehives that Saturday morning,
the wind chasing the waves against them in white furls, in longships.
When the bees furred into the air at last
they hung in a cloud, a circle of smoke,
audible even above the blunder of the sea against the rocks.
And the boy breathed the salt and the wind –
felt brave, felt big.

OTTER

In a furrow of bubbles once –
he became –
the ever-flowing curve of a thing
that can never be still,
from the first stirrings of pink
when morning lies in the window of the east
like a new-caught salmon, he's off:
sewn out of rivers and hills, a bend of grace –
his nose telling ten thousand tales,
everything listening inside, eager
to be under and over and through
this element he can never let go –
born out of water,
water made otter.

SALT AND LIGHT

The child comes back home at evening full of stories;
they're spoken in a dry and salty torrent like a rush of silver fish;
pour onto the kitchen table where the faraway blue,
the afterglow of sun still are. She takes his hands in hers;
sits him at the table and wipes the sand from one eyebrow,
and touches the place on his left knee with its little cut of blood
and she thinks that all this is why life means so much.

Honestly

I have searched for God
in the dry echoes of tall stone buildings
where the laws are written dark upon the walls.

I have found God
in the broken bread of light across the moorland,
as it silvers from the miracle of the earth.

SABBATH

Even now the word glooms my heart –
takes the football, the climbing of trees from my boy's heart
and puts them under lock and key.
The high clock ticks. Black curtains drape the windows,
block out the June blue skies, the rejoicing of birds.
At ten years young, God seemed to me
like a heavy implement intent on hurting.
My mother's people far back across the misty hills of time
buried their fiddles and songs in the moors,
burned every vestige of celebration
lest the dark scowl of their church heard tell of it
and brought down hell.
But still, just sometimes, on a Sabbath, I slipped out
to the forbidden early morning singing of the dawn.

BUTTERFLY

All winter folded in a cupboard
boarded away among coats
in the musty darkness of a cupboard.
Until today. It flies out, soft as eyelids,
unfolds a latticework of wings –
patters the windowsill to be free.
Outside the thrushes dripping songs from the bushes;
a rainbow smudging thickly over town
in the slow wetness of a Thursday afternoon in March.
I creak the handle till I open
a thin corner of sky. I watch a miracle help
this little piece of summer into light.

THREADS

Something there is in going over grass at break of light.
Look back and see the silver passage of your feet
like grey ghosts through the green.
But even bare feet softly left in grass will mark out time,
will break the dew, may risk the spider's web fragility of light –
just sometimes, watch. Let soft fingers of your senses
touch and take the little pieces of the morning's gifts
to store for times of hunger, to last you through the winter dark.

JUNE

Barefoot the stairs, sigh your hand gently
down the smooth wood of the banister,
and stand at ten in the morning listening
to the blue song of the house.

All the doors are open and light
moves between rooms like a half-asleep child;
there is no hurry, time passes so slow
you can hear it breathe in the curtains.

SUILVEN

We were below the head of Suilven
on a day thundered with cloud,
above a loch and the blown crests of its waves –
when suddenly we heard the loons calling and stretching,
aching over wide water, their voices carrying
eerie and long, beautiful, a whole language
borne by the wind of that early August
so we had to stop and listen, our own words
blown away forgotten.
Who knows how long we stayed, beyond time,
a little of our lives lost and left behind,
listening to the loons.

BENBECULA

An island flattened to the wind,
a flimsy thing in the Atlantic –
where colors come at once
out of the middle of everywhere.

When morning breaks each darkness
it turns more loch than land;
a moon of rocks and pools
as far as the eye can carry.

The lochs lie in that land
like watercolour lines,
such a frail blue they're light
scuttering with the calls of birds.

A lark grace-notes the dawn
spinning notes from the sky,
unravelling the tangle of clouds
that are ceaselessly blowing away.

I reach the rim of the sea
that's breaking in sudden hushes,
and I know what I have come to find
is just as ever it was –

always changing and always still the same.

WHITHORN

Late in July
light is yellow-blue and the last
lingers under trees in lemoning.

Somehow time melts,
does not matter,
means nothing.

And this could be
that night the monks
clustered from Ireland in their coracles.

Lamps limping fields –
in the blue ghost of dark
a bell echoing midnight.

A barn owl flutters through softness;
a moon struggles upwards, huge and full,
climbs to light the fields.

Then and now melded
in a place that happens sometimes
late in July.

ST. KILDA

Always in winter the fiddle tunes came
when the wind shone bright on the headlands;
grazing the eye, battling the house at night –
mad and almighty.

He lay there, in the small hours before dawn came;
and the Atlantic swelled the room, bringing in its fingers
stories of far away, of long ago,
of make-believe.

And the notes swam into his hands;
they chased and danced, little chinks of things,
till he heard them, till they crammed his head
with a whole symphony of song.

He took his fiddle and he fought for them;
listened, his ear catching the Atlantic,
searching and sifting the right note
before it faded lost for ever.

By the time morning had blown back from the sea,
lay grey and dazed in the window,
the tune was done, was drying,
like a fish net in the wind.

LIGHT

Sometimes I wonder
why I drag west again and again
back along pot-holed roads
into a splintering of summer rain,
and the house is rattled all night long
like a rat in a terrier's mouth by gale.
Yet always next morning
it's quiet that comes to waken me;
a lark spinning somewhere in torn sky,
and in the corner of my window
an orchid with a yellow head
nods in a sanctuary of rocks.
And there, up there, a loch so blue
lies in the claws of the hills
like a sapphire held in a brooch,
blowing with lilies.
I come back here blessed, time after time,
my hands full of all I had lost.

MOONSHINE

The moon is a bloated bag of mercury
swelling and spilling across the night.

The light comes down across the water
like a shoal of electric eels.

The moon is the head of a very old man,
the polished fossil of his skull.

Bits of it fall, become the faces
of barn owls ghosting over fields.

But in the water-blue sky of day,
the moon is a rag-nail and nothing at all.

GEESE

This evening I went out with a basket of clothes
to hang to dry in the wind. Above the wood
I saw a silver brooch of moon
molten through the trees in fierce blue nightfall.
I heard them first. A hundred thousand
ragged voices clamouring against the wind;
I stopped what I was doing to look up, listen,
knowing somehow this was bigger.
I saw them – a rippling of backs, of wings,
that caught the moon and made waves of its light,
like the quicksilver of the Atlantic's ripples
across a white shell beach.
I listened to them until the sky had taken them
and even then I listened, a towel hanging from my hand.
All night I've listened to the memory of their passing, lost,
as the washing billows ghostly in the moonlight, wind-blown.

How Things Seem

This is not a poem about kingfishers
but rather some place off the beaten track;
a slither of water among the reeds in dimness
and the heavy smell of thick mud.
It is about the argument, the whining,
that had to do with getting up at six to trail here
into the middle of nowhere and for nothing.

This is not a poem about kingfishers;
how a blue-green heart of bird
flowed through grey air a whole moment
barely above the water,
then turned perfect back to gemstone;
one little fist of opalescence
held by a single stem.

RETURN

Summer has come back like a swallow from Africa.
On the blue-pale mussel shell evenings
when the stars come out to play
it is too warm; there is too much blue to sleep
when all winter we will sit
behind the rattle of grey windows wishing.
Take a heavy chair onto the terrace
in the mauve shadows of eleven o'clock
and feel the moths fur against your face.
Across the lake the last lamps of houses
drift, ruffled and patterned.
A plane humming somewhere up above,
slow as an insect, its one eye winking.
The skies are thundery, in the far east
lightning like gold thread
hangs from the curtains of a theatre
and exits at last stage left.

GOD

Sunday rang out over the valley
and I walked into the wild cathedral of the hills.
I took off my shoes to feel the flowers
as they sang in the wind. I put my hands into the stream's voice
to feel the healing white of its cut.

I listened at the top of the valley:
God was there in the green glass of the place
like a feather against my heart –
the part of me that is missing,
that I am always looking to find.

THE BREAD OF LIFE

Father, you put good things in our mouths
and open sky upon our shoulders. You grew the grass
between our unshod feet and blew a haystack fire of sun
to wake the summer. You gave us barns for childhood;
rainbows we could run and never catch,
and otters in their flowing laughter through the streams.
You gave us goose-soft snow outside the window
and deep Decembers for the rush of sledges,
till green days sang the trees again, and birdsong dripped
another year upon the pages of our eyes.
And when I see the stained glass window of the sky,
I thank you, Father, for the bread of life you broke.

II

COLUMBA

A film lies across the water meadows
like a muslin shawl. Birds lament
among rushes, their low voices trailing
like beads of glass. The sun has not been born yet,
remains under woods and hills.
Columba goes down, his ankles buried by soft water,
by green fronds, slippery, making no more sound
than a deer. The swans drift over the water,
so white they hurt the eyes. He stops,
forgetting everything as he watches the stoop and silver
of their grace, the sudden rippling of their backs
cast by wind, the furling of the huge wings
like shards of ice. They too are prayers,
personified, awakenings of God
in the morning water land.
He goes on, to the strange stone head
carved and lying dormant in the grass;
those wide eyes that never blinked,
the ringlets of stone hair curling
about the enigma of a half-buried face.
He comes here, even though the smiths who cut this
have known only gods of wood and loam,
have chanted under the wheels of stars,
made strange offerings of wheat and fire and gold.
Here at the water meadow's end he finds the Christ
ripe in his heart, his lips brim with words
that soar like larks into the sky,

almost as if some spring of light and joy
wells from the ground beneath.
He kneels in the wet softness of the earth
and smells the springtime yellow in his veins –
becomes the place he prays in.

CLONMACNOISE

Wrapped in the wool of winter,
the fields breathed with frost;

even the Shannon confused
searching in ribbons through the fields –

the sun straining to see
like a single frozen eye.

We came to Clonmacnoise
fifteen hundred years too late:

crows in the ivied silence of round towers,
gravestones bent as though in penitence;

chapels fallen in upon themselves
like broken faith –

and yet I could imagine
in the once upon a time of Ireland

men awakening to break the wells,
to bring in steamings of white water;

keeping the turf fire's glow
storm after December storm

here where they had caught God's light
(so fragile, yet alive for ever)

to bear it bright
out into the dark places of the earth.

THE ILLUMINATED MANUSCRIPT

They brought me here from Ireland, still a boy
to begin their book.

I remember the day I left –
soft bread, a silvering of geese, the sound of my mother.

Now I slip the stone of these steps every day
long before dawn, breathe the dark

and hear the whelming of the winds about this fastness
before my one candle like a petal of gorse

flutters the shadows in ghosts over the cold walls.
Out of the thin window I watch the sea all winter

heave and drag like a dying man,
the skies blackened and bruised.

Some days there is nothing in the pen except
my own emptiness; I hold it hoping

until the stars blow out from the attic of the skies
and a ledge of moon lifts across the hills.

Just sometimes something breaks inside
like the brittle lid of a casket

and pours out light onto the waiting page.

SOLACE

I look back through my mind and see
the days when forest wolved the land in mystery
and light was cradled out of coracles
in wild and wintered island storm.

All night and every night the rip and snarl of wind,
and this their task alone, to guard the light they had been given –
the flutter of that single flame
keeping out the whole world of the dark.

THE HERMIT'S CELL

I had to listen for a silence
that was born inside.

It took a whole year to find
and now it does not fail.

I need nothing;
all I want is where I am.

I used to pray, and praying then
was struggle with myself.

Now I am made prayer, am hollowed out –
a song that needs no sound.

I pick the blow of flowers, bring them back
in blues and reds and golds,

and in the slow of winter dark
I watch for dawn and know

that I am growing into light
a little every day.

ISLAND

We came to the island
reluctant, dragged our feet
up over the gravel.

Three nights we remained
in the monastery's rattling emptiness –
our heads shorn cold, ears echoing song.

The wind came like scurrying creatures
gnawing at fingers and feet;
milk-blue moonlight filled the cloisters.

We prayed, and at first our prayers
were ragged things, torn thoughts
that blew into the fierce dark.

Then in the waking pain of the second night
something broke the jar of my heart;
a softness flowed I had not known before.

On the third day I walked to the south end,
met the sea leaping in fierce dogs –
my hands felt skiffed like flints.

But not only my hands.
I came back from the island, all of us came back
glass vessels, see-through, clear.

THE DEATH OF COLUMBA

It was another day. The bell echoed;
a coracle came with news of Ireland
and a fine cut of meat. The sea
wrapped round the island like a mantle of silk.

Everything he did as always, just a beat slower.
They saw nothing; the talk was generous,
the laughter easy, as a lark spun songs
somewhere out of sky that still morning.

Yet the horse came. In the middle of it all,
and the faces turned like full moons
as that long head rested on his shoulder
and the nostrils, full of hay, flared.

For the horse had heard
dark in the drumbeat of his heart
that edge of death, and wept
softly against the old man's head.

Salt tears like the water that had brought him once
out of the heart of Ireland,
that would take him now
over a last sea, into the land he had lived.

PLACE

And God said:
Let there be a place made of stone
out off the west of the world;
roughed nine months by gale,
rattled in Atlantic swell.

A place that rouses each Easter
with soft blessings of flowers
and shocks of white shell sand;
a place found only sometimes
by those who have lost their way.

IONA FERRY

It's the smell I remember –
the dizziness of diesel, tarry rope, wood sheened like toffee.
The sea was waving in the wind, a dancing –
I wanted it to be rough and yet I didn't.
My mother and I snugged under the awning
to a dark rocking. We were low as the waves;
all of us packed in tight like bales of wool.
The engine roared alive, its tremor
juddered through the wood and thrilled me, beat my heart.
The shore began fading behind the white curl of our hum.
Fourteen days lay barefoot on the island –
still asleep, their eyes all shut.
And yet I knew them all already,
felt them in my pocket like polished stones –
their orchids, their hurt-white sand, their larksong.

COLL

I remember what it was like to barefoot that house,
wood rooms bleached by light. Days were new voyages, journeys,
coming home a pouring out of stories and of starfish.
The sun never died completely in the night;
the skies just turned luminous, the wind
tugged at the strings in the grass like a hand
in a harp. I did not sleep, too glad to listen by a window
to the sorrow sounds of the birds
as they swept down in skeins, and rose again, celebrating
all that was summer. I did not sleep, the weight of school
behind and before too great to waste a grain of this.
One four in the morning at first larksong – I went west over the dunes,
broke down running onto three miles of white shell sand and stood.
A wave curled and silked the shore in a single seamless breath.
I went naked into the water, ran deep into a green
through which I was translucent. I rejoiced
in something I could not name; I celebrated a wonder
too huge to hold. I trailed home, slow and golden,
dried by the sunlight.

IONA

Is this place really nearer to God?
Is the wall thin between our whispers
and his listening? I only know
the world grows less and less –
here what matters is conquering the wind,
coming home dryshod, getting the fire lit.
I am not sure whether there is no time here
or more time, whether the light is stronger
or just easier to see. That is why
I keep returning, thirsty, to this place
that is older than my understanding,
younger than my broken spirit.

A LARK

A handful of lark
buoyant on the strings of a summer morning
twirling and spinning songs
overtures and symphonies
though it has learned no music
in the schools of London or Paris
but is sight-reading instead
the kettledrums of the Atlantic
the white bells of the orchids
the violins of the wind.

THE WELL

I found a well once
in the dark green heart of a wood

where pigeons ruffled up into a skylight of branches
and disappeared.

The well was old, so mossed and broken
it was almost a part of the wood

gone back to nature. Carefully, almost fearfully,
I looked down into its depths

and saw the lip of water shifting and tilting,
heard the music of dripping stones.

I stretched down, cupped a deep handful
out of the winter darkness of its world

and drank. That water tasted of moss, of secrets,
of ancient meetings, of laughter,

of dark stone, of crystal –
it reached the roots of my being

assuaged a whole summer of thirst.
I have been wandering for that water ever since.

PRAYER

If you do not believe in God
go on a blue spring day across these fields:
listen to the orchids, race the sea, scent the wind.

Come back and tell it was all an accident
a collision of blind chance
in the empty hugeness of space.

THE SMALL GIANT

The otter is ninety percent water
ten percent God.

This is a mastery
we have not fathomed in a million years.

I saw one once, off the teeth of western Scotland,
playing games with the Atlantic –

Three feet of gymnastics
taking on an ocean.

WEST

Leave Craignure and the woods around Duart Castle
and hug the shore before you climb the lion-colored hills:
Glengorm, from which the people once were burned.
Up higher and still higher, until the lochs lie far below
and if you're lucky, the whole bald head of Ben More
has broken out of cloud and stares west, a weathered sphinx.
A telephone box, a single house, and miles of salt marsh
for the constant hope of otters. Then on, to Pennyghael,
and the thin single road that winds like a piece of thread
over to the cliffs of Carsaig. But keep on heading west,
until Bunessan and the harbour and the clustered houses.
You're almost there. An inland loch, impossibly blue,
and now the breeze blows every way at once –
the land lies low, left with a few wind-twisted trees,
and see, ahead, there, on the edge of the sky,
the island still at anchor; the abbey nestled by the sea –
guarding, keeping, waiting.

THE THIN PLACE

People have come here for centuries
to rearrange the stones, to make sense of the silence
they cannot catch and keep for the journey back.
They find here something of all they are missing
in the real world (that is somehow not real anymore).
They wish they had come here before, sooner,
to see it over there, on the edge of the sky,
where a late sun is blessing the sea.

Lamb

I found a lamb,
tugged by the guyropes of the wind,
trying so hard to get up.

It was no more than a trembling bundle –
a bag of bones and wet wool,
a voice made of crying, like a child's.

What a beginning, what a fall,
to be born here on the edge of the world
between the sea and America.

Lamb, out of this island of stone
yellow is coming, golden promises,
the buttery sunlight of spring.

ADMISSION

I can never take a photograph of a whole place:
all that is possible is a piece, a part –
there will always be something that is lost, left out.
I could capture the fire with flames dancing the coals,
but not the scent of this small room –
smoke and peat and whisky mixed together;
nor could I turn and take
the whole sea listing and swilling between islands,
or the picture of a tallow-coloured boat
battling across with the low hum of an engine.
I could never catch completely
the skies clearing and the late October light
coming sometimes in a hurrying –
brightness and bleakness
in their play of change for ever.

SERPENTINE

A little cave of green stone
smoothed by centuries of sea
to a pebble small as a pinkie nail
chanced up out of the waves' reach.
Hold it to light and it changes,
becomes a globe of fractures;
a cavern of ledges and glinting –
not one green but many at once.
And suddenly I think of it bigger
as the whole of the human heart;
carrying the cuts of its journey –
brokenness letting in light.

THE BAY AT THE BACK OF THE OCEAN

I come back here brittle and broken,
to be washed up new and rinsed and clean;
with eyes that no longer see
the clutter of what needs to be done.

To be made pure west again
on days the sea's moiling and searching;
roaring over beaches in chariots,
beneath the battlefield of the skies.

Then when the light comes, sometimes,
shimmering like a whole shoal of herring,
and the wind stands still, I think –
this is to fill the heart.

SALT

When you have forgotten what it means
to have the wind hurrying your window all night long
it's time to find the island. There is a gate –
beyond, a track that's made of sand
winding down the *machair*. You'll hear the sea
long before you're there, or the shoulders of the island
have opened so that all the horses of the west
are galloping the beach, again and now again.
And if you should open too and let in light,
it is because the breakages within you are so many,
and the salt, no matter how it hurts, will heal.

LOGIE

When I was a boy I went every Saturday
to the north end of the island –
to her farmhouse for eggs.

I walked against the wind
that was full of snowflakes
the salt knife of the sea.

When I got to her doorway
the collies flowed out at me
black and white bounces of barking.

She brought me into her home
gave me six eggs in a box
to take back for the coming week.

Last night her son was drowned
returning in a boat at midnight –
he was lost and will not come home.

I am older and have been far away
in different corners of the world –
I have seen all that I expected.

But now I am returning to the island
I am going to the north end
to the woman who once gave me eggs.

And when I get there and the collies come round me
and I stand in the kitchen and see her
a whole ocean will drown me.

DOVES

Talking with the man on the bus
from Iona to the end of Mull,
and thinking of his white papers for defence
that had fluttered like doves from Whitehall –
I still told him where the otters were
and the relics of the Gaelic poets,
thinking how small he would be
playing God with a chessboard of figures,
bombs at his disposal,
in some lonely corridor of power
where something as lovely as a sunset
or the crying of a curlew
would never come.

HEBRIDES

This shattered place, this place of fragments,
a play of wind and sea and light;
shifting always, becoming and diminishing –
out of nowhere the full brightness of morning
blown away, buried and lost.

And yet, if you have faith, if you wait long enough,
there will be the miracle of an otter
turning water into somersaults;
the jet blackness of a loch brought back to life
by the sudden touch of sun.

But you will take nothing home with you
save your own changedness,
and this wind that will waken you
sometimes, all your life, yearning to return.

III

THE WOODPECKER

All day it rained, that last day of May.
The streets were scoured, shining and silver.
At three I heard the *yaffle* of a woodpecker
far away, and went outside to stand listening
under the music of the rain. All I heard now
was the *dunt* of my own heart. I took my jacket,
walked into the wood on soft feet
beneath trees wide as horses. Again I listened,
whole symphonies of rain were falling:
the air was thatched with birdsong –
a jewellery of flutes – but no woodpecker.
Down below, the early summer river
went by like dark green glass.
Wet scents of flowers, ferns, mushrooms, grass
thickened my breath. I just walked
until I was shining and silver myself, made of rain.
I found everything I had been looking for,
except what I'd set out to find.

The Summer House

The window opens so the wind
blooms through the lit rooms.
The doors breathe, and upstairs
the curtains in the bedrooms are all closed
so the cool is kept till the dark returns.
I remember my childhood home
and the oranges there on the kitchen table –
hot glows of softness. I smelled them
and closed my eyes to a journey:
the faraway blue of sky and sea
and trees that were heavy with fruit.
Summer is the corns of sand in my shoes;
a garden warm with easy talk –
night and the windows breathing free.

SOMEHOW

I do not want the world
I cannot understand.
I want instead
a place that is inside myself.
I see through a dark window
sometimes, to its possibility,
on warm summer evenings
when all the light is honey
and the people graze in flocks
among the fields
talking about betrothals as their barbecues
spit and bubble, and the river
slides away in one single
stained glass window to the sea.

MOTHER

As though my mother were in a boat
drifting a little further all the time;
her answers slow over distant water
and her eyes coming into focus gradually –
as though seeing in black and white
not frozen photographs of brittle paper
but rather going back into their landscape,
telling me things I must remember –
not about now and the meaningless world
that spins its insanity about us –
but the world she came from,
that I must take from the water carefully
like glass buoys, delicate and darkly shining,
before we forget who we were for ever.

FATHER

Three days you have been gone
and still the mornings feel stunned.
The thrushes spill huge vases of song on the lawn
in early morning rain, the spring skies hurt
like vulnerable skin. We move about the house
conscious of your absence – listening to it,
carrying it, touching it. A huge sea keeps catching me
off-balance; great waves sweep away my feet,
my eyes. And in the morning I lie washed up
on an endless white shore, empty,
do not recognise my own reflection.

I knot the black tie at my throat
and cannot swallow. All morning
I practise pleasantries, rehearse a smile that hurts.
At the crematorium in the soft organ chords
and the over-pink flowers
I cannot find you anywhere at all.
There is so much I wish I could forget to remember;
this is a wound that always changes places.
I did not say goodbye to you
and so I'll go on trying to find the words
all the rest of my life.

FAREWELL

Twinkles of things
dimpling and flocking
this silver-blue night;
the last of summer
in their tassles, those dark streamers –
restless to swim the skies to Africa.
They take the year with them in their wings,
and all they leave behind
are the crinkled lanes of autumn:
the galed nights, the huge moon
riding through piles of cloud.
Father, you who waited for the first swallow
each new summer;
who longed for their swivelled grace
in the high roofs of the morning –
now it is you who have gone
long before the swallows,
and though I'll miss you all the winter long
spring will not bring you back.

STOPPING TO SEE

When the land is rusting
and the wind's returned
to ruffle the water so it's cold and sore
under the eyes, and the sun
comes but seldom and when it does,
the sea is flooded but above
the sky's left dark and angry –
then head against the wind
and walk until you have stopped thinking
of all you've left behind, the tasks
that still need doing. You are blown out,
have gone beyond all clocks and watches
into a place where only being matters.
No-one has seen the world through your eyes before
and you stop, breathless, to be given
the moment whooper swans come down as soft as silk
across the surface of a loch,
and just above, the low moon's
like a ball of cobwebs in the ice-blue skies
and you know, without a doubt,
there could not be anything
so beautiful again.

NIGHT

At night the world is not what it was;
beyond the lights everything ends,
a door of blackness bangs. I hear the wood,
rising and falling in the wind like a huge sea,
but it is utterly dark. At night it is not ours –
neither tamed nor pathed nor fenced –
it is we who are, in our small boxed worlds,
alone and left afraid.

HINDS

They are there in the darkness,
in the warm night and the warm shadows;
such big softness you must hold your breath
to know they're there at all. In lamplight they loom large –
the budded tips of their antlers jagging the air,
eyes lemoned in the light.

You break a branch
and they've leapt away
vanished as soft as thistledown;
gone into the umber night as one,
the fields left eerie and empty behind them
as a gourd of moon spills from the opened dark.

INSTRUCTIONS FOR AUTUMN

Let the breeze come and fill the wood;
watch the copper-coloured leaves cloud the air
in a moment's sudden light.

Cross a fence and walk down the edge of a field
beside the white exuberance of an October stream
full of bounce, incoherent with whole days of rain.

There they are. Ten or a dozen trees
who knows how old, all hazels,
leaves freckled with edges of rust.

Clusters of chestnuts swaying above your head –
here and here, and right up there!
Catch their crackling bunches, rattle them into the bag.

Make time for the thudding of your boots
down the old farm track; slush through muddy pools
and watch for the first geese in the field.

THE OTHER SHEPHERD

I stayed. Someone had to.
Three in the morning and the cold
like a rusty knife. The fire down to a dragon's eye;
a cave that glowed. The whole globe of the moon
broke into the skies' maroon hugeness;
lit them, sliding and glittering
down towards the sleep of the town
clasped in the crook of the hills.
Then nothing. The wind breathed, blew the moon away.
A whole two hours I watched, listening to the dark
huge about me, till the fire
gusted into a rubble of dust.
Then without warning they were back in a babble
with some story big as a fisherman's brag,
eyes wide with its size:
it poured loud and confused as coins
scatter from a bag.
I nodded and smiled;
curled round into the blanket of night
and closed my eyes –
they'd have forgotten all about it by morning.

SIGHT

Christmas is gone, the wet skies hurry by;
the ash grey and claggy in the grate.
The houses round about lie fast asleep,
half-way through morning.

In Bethlehem, the visitors have gone –
lost interest for another year.
They slope away, looking for bigger stars and gifts,
tired of standing watching what they cannot see.

THE WINTER OF 2010

Three weeks this winter –
nights minus twenty, anchored in the cold.

The sun is made of snow;
below, a finery of frost on all the world.

Ponds like the eyes of dead men,
their light all gone and glazed.

The hills whispered soft with white
seem higher, wilder than they really are.

Two swans swim the sky,
the horns of their necks stretched north.

A flock of birds scatters from the trees,
nothing more than glints in grey air.

There are geese in patches on the fields,
wandering and wondering, loudly.

Words come from mouths
misshapen, numb and slow.

All our roads closed, snowed-in –
we have gone back to the beginning.

The Hills in the Window

The farm has not changed.
Its Christmas windows welcomed me
when I was two feet smaller.
The granddaughter of the first collie I knew
bounces out to meet me, a flow of black and white.

We are all of us older
but the hands are no less warm;
the friendship and talk as rich,
as precious as in the beginning –
the hills in the window will always remain.

THE ROAD

Now we are hard of hearing. The big world
thunders in our ears and gives us
all that we do not need. Just sometimes
a young deer turns in the early morning frost
and we see, for a moment, the beautiful road,
that lies like an ache in our blood.

THE LAND

The fields lie unploughed now –
we have bartered them for nothing more than bigger towns.
Our farms lie semi-derelict;
places that stare back at us from motorways.

We have forgotten how to read the land and thrown away
long years of learning. The bright machines
that bought our hearts
hummed sweeter songs in their dumb blades.

But in the turning of the seasons there was bread
that broke a joy in those who knew the land,
who felt its hold. We have forgotten
what that ground was like beneath our feet.

Is this the place we prayed for,
or have we gone too far?
We were not meant to carry more than we could hold,
and now we cannot see the way that might lead back.

GOOD FRIDAY

The Cross melts; from it weeps candle-wax,
and in its hive of light the women's faces bend
lined with their years of prayer.

The Christ seems still alive, as if the drops of blood and sweat
were there and wet; a few soft footsteps from our kneeling
the tears shining from his eyes.

Two thousand years are dead; we cross a strange river
to that Calvary, our lives imprinted
with the wood and nails of Easter.

RESURRECTION

I

I watched from hideaways
when pigeons softened into white air.
He spoke, his voice soft as bread –
I listened in the shadows.
I too lay awake when rumour ran
like scuttling white-eyed rats among the nights.
We ate in whispers,
frightened of everything.
And I was there when they dragged him away
in the flickering torchlight of darkness.
I think he loved me too.

II

Judas was dead; found in a field,
his eyes huge and pieces of shining
scattered about his feet.
Peter gibbering and half-mad, unslept –
wandering the streets like a drunk,
his eyes sore with grief.
Pilate standing at a window,
his wet hands searching for something
they could never find again.
The city thundery and anxious, waiting –
eyes listening for movement
behind closed doors.
Only the women softly sharing his words;
tenderly remembering them like prayers
in the hour before dawn on the Sabbath.

III

They waited and the net was empty.
The skill of fish had fled their hands
as life had left their master's.
The carpenter dead with wood and nails:
Rome had hammered home an old message.
Day broke bloody and sore;
they came ashore, cold and hungry.
Light tried and failed. A lone tree
red and hurting in the wind
and someone waiting on the shore.

HIS DISCIPLES

Brave cowards,
they followed the man from Galilee
up hill and down while the crowds sang and exulted
over healed hands and blessed children.
Till a dark ripple of thunder fissured the sky
like a viper's tongue. Those in high places
whispered ugly about the man and the wild dance
of those who followed his every footstep, his slightest command.
They pounced at last. With wood and nails
they made certain that the miracle would be stamped out
to the last breath. Silence reigned for three days;
his disciples scuttled into darkness, hid like mice.
But the wood grew roots, flowered, blossomed –
rose at last once more
into the hands and feet of the carpenter.
His followers crept out into the sunlight of his rising.
And later, after he had gone back to God
strange fire lit them and took the small fear of their lives;
hammered them strong and silver, brighter than suns –
set them alight to rampage the earth with good news.

IMAGINE

Imagine waking one morning
and hearing nothing but birdsong;
going outside into stunned sunlight –
a rush hour that isn't there.

No planes overhead, no lorries
thundering north and south
with anger in their wheels.

On the television screen
just a white blizzard of hissing;
no voice assuring you that everything
will be back in place by midday.

And when you listen to that silence
will you miss what's gone for good?
Will it frighten you that the old order
has been swept away like snow
with the back of a single hand?

Or is there somewhere deep inside
secretly rejoicing
that this is beginning again?

In Michigan

All day we went north and north;
crossed the bridge to the Upper Peninsula.

And there was something older there,
an America everyone forgets –
and the woods grew around us,
and the blue glass of Lake Superior
played and glanced in the white May light.

And we came to a place called Paradise
and there was no more motorway –
just a slowness to smiling and kindness
I'd all but forgotten, that we have left behind
in our rush to get somewhere we don't want to be.
There was birdsong in the trees, the laughter of children –
the blue of the sky and the blue of the lake.

The world was made of many blues
and I wanted to take off my shoes.

Remembering the Amish

And I have seen them coming home on summer nights
or bent above the washbowl in the kitchen,
haloed in the window by the low sun's leaving;
soft voices in the fields of gentle men with horses.

And in the town they walk their own way,
as though a reverence for what lies beneath their feet
is in their shoes, and in their eyes a peace
no man may buy and few have ever found.

And sometimes when I meet them I feel like him who went
with all his father's wealth and lived in laughter far away
and woke one day to find he'd nothing left.
I feel like turning just like him for home –

That I may also start again.

THE SACRED PLACE

I want to be there but I cannot reach
through the window to the high hills
where snow has lain for weeks –
a shield smoothed now in sunlight,
glinting. Yet if I were there
I would bring the weight of myself
made of so many mistakes
and it would not be any longer.
Sometimes it is enough
to see the perfect place
and keep the snow unbroken.

SHORT GLOSSARY
of SCOTTISH GAELIC WORDS AND PLACES

Benbecula: small island in the Outer Hebrides

Ben More: highest mountain on the Isle of Mull, often visible from Iona

Bunessan: village on the Isle of Mull

Carsaig: bay and cove on the south coast of the Isle of Mull

Clonmacnoise: sixth-century monastery on the River Shannon in Ireland

Coll: island of the Inner Hebrides

Craignure: main ferry port on the Isle of Mull

dunt: bump

Glengorm: castle on the Isle of Mull

Luskentyre: scattered settlement on the Isle of Harris in the Outer Hebrides, with beaches renowned for their white shell sand

machair: rich grass that grows at the top of Hebridean beaches

Mull: the second-largest island of the Inner Hebrides, off which Iona lies

Pennyghael: village in the Ross of Mull, the long southern arm of the Isle of Mull

Suilven: iconic mountain in Sutherland, north-west Scotland

Whithorn: site of the first Christian church in Scotland in the late fourth century, established by Saint Ninian

yaffle: the onomatopoeic sound of the great spotted woodpecker

ABOUT PARACLETE PRESS

WHO WE ARE

As the publishing arm of the Community of Jesus, Paraclete Press presents a full expression of Christian belief and practice—from Catholic to Evangelical, from Protestant to Orthodox, reflecting the ecumenical charism of the Community and its dedication to sacred music, the fine arts, and the written word. We publish books, recordings, sheet music, and video/DVDs that nourish the vibrant life of the church and its people.

WHAT WE ARE DOING

BOOKS | PARACLETE PRESS BOOKS show the richness and depth of what it means to be Christian. While Benedictine spirituality is at the heart of who we are and all that we do, our books reflect the Christian experience across many cultures, time periods, and houses of worship.

We have many series, including *Paraclete Essentials*; *Paraclete Fiction*; *Paraclete Poetry*; *Paraclete Giants*; and for children and adults, *All God's Creatures*, books about animals and faith; and *San Damiano Books*, focusing on Franciscan spirituality. Others include *Voices from the Monastery* (men and women monastics writing about living a spiritual life today), *Active Prayer*, and new for young readers: *The Pope's Cat*. We also specialize in gift books for children on the occasions of Baptism and First Communion, as well as other important times in a child's life, and books that bring creativity and liveliness to any adult spiritual life.

The MOUNT TABOR BOOKS series focuses on the arts and literature as well as liturgical worship and spirituality; it was created in conjunction with the Mount Tabor Ecumenical Centre for Art and Spirituality in Barga, Italy.

MUSIC | PARACLETE PRESS DISTRIBUTES RECORDINGS of the internationally acclaimed choir *Gloriæ Dei Cantores*, the *Gloriæ Dei Cantores Schola*, and the other instrumental artists of the *Arts Empowering Life Foundation*.

PARACLETE PRESS IS THE EXCLUSIVE NORTH AMERICAN DISTRIBUTOR for the Gregorian chant recordings from St. Peter's Abbey in Solesmes, France. Paraclete also carries all of the Solesmes chant publications for Mass and the Divine Office, as well as their academic research publications.

In addition, PARACLETE PRESS SHEET MUSIC publishes the work of today's finest composers of sacred choral music, annually reviewing over 1,000 works and releasing between 40 and 60 works for both choir and organ.

VIDEO | Our video/DVDs offer spiritual help, healing, and biblical guidance for a broad range of life issues including grief and loss, marriage, forgiveness, facing death, understanding suicide, bullying, addictions, Alzheimer's, and Christian formation.

Learn more about us at our website:
www.paracletepress.com
or phone us toll-free at 1.800.451.5006

SCAN
TO
READ

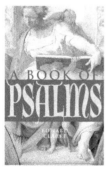

9 781640 606302